Lourdes Christian Gospel Rosary Prayer Book

(Full Color Large Print)

By Laus Deo

www.lausdeopublishing.org

Laus Deo - "Praise be to God"

Table of Contents

1) Our Lady of Lourdes

The pilgrimage of Lourdes is founded on the apparitions of the Blessed Virgin to a poor, fourteen-year-old girl, Bernadette Soubiroux. The first apparition occurred 11 February, 1858. There were eighteen in all; the last took place 16 July, of the same year. Bernadette often fell into an ecstasy. The mysterious vision she saw in the hollow of the rock Massabielle was that of a young and beautiful lady. "Lovelier than I have ever seen" said the child. But the girl was the only one who saw the vision, although sometimes many stood there with her. Now and then the apparition spoke to the seer who also was the only one who heard the voice. Thus, she one day told her to drink of a mysterious fountain, in the grotto itself, the existence of which was unknown, and of which there was no sign, but which immediately gushed forth. On another occasion the apparition bade Bernadette go and tell the priests she wished a chapel to be built on the spot and processions to be made to the grotto. At first the clergy were incredulous. It was only four years later, in 1862, that the bishop of the diocese declared the faithful "justified in believing the reality of the apparition". A basilica was built upon the rock of Massabielle by M. Peyramale, the parish priest. In 1873 the great "national" French pilgrimages were inaugurated. Three years later the basilica was consecrated and the statue solemnly crowned. In 1883 the foundation stone of another church was laid, as the first was no longer large enough. It was built at the foot of the basilica and was consecrated in 1901 and called the Church of the Rosary. Pope Leo XIII authorized a special office and a Mass, in commemoration of the apparition, and in 1907 Pius X extended the observance of this feast to the entire Church; it is now observed on 11 February.

Never has a sanctuary attracted such throngs. At the end of the year 1908, when the fiftieth anniversary of the apparition was celebrated, although the record really only began from 1867, 5297 pilgrimages had been registered and these had brought 4,919,000 pilgrims. Individual pilgrims are more numerous by far than those who come in groups. To their number must be added the visitors who do not come as pilgrims, but who are attracted by a religious feeling or sometimes merely by the desire to see this far-famed spot. The Company of the Chemins de Fer du Midi estimates that the Lourdes station receives over one million travellers per annum. Every nation in the world furnishes its contingent. Out of the total of pilgrimages given above, four hundred and sixty-four came from countries other than France. They are sent by the United States, Germany, Belgium, Austria, Hungary, Spain, Portugal, Italy, England, Ireland, Canada, Brazil, Bolivia, etc. The bishops lead the way. At the end of the year of the fiftieth anniversary, 2013 prelates, including 546 archbishops, 10 primates, 19 patriarchs, 69 cardinals, had made the pilgrimage to Lourdes. But more remarkable still than the crowd of pilgrims is the series of wonderful occurrences which take place under the protection of the celebrated sanctuary. Passing over spiritual cures, which more often than not escape human observance, we shall confine ourselves to bodily diseases. The writer of this article has recorded every recovery, whether partial or complete, and in the first half-century of the shrine's existence he has counted 3962. Notwithstanding very careful statistics which give the names and surnames of the patients who have recovered, the date of the cure, the name of the disease, and generally that of the physician who had charge of the case, there are inevitably doubtful or mistaken cases, attributable, as a rule, to the excited fancy of the afflicted one and which time soon dispels. But it is only right to note: first, that these unavoidable errors regard only secondary cases which have not like the others been the object of special study; it must also be noted that the number of cases is equalled and exceeded by actual cures which are not put on record. The afflicted who have recovered are not obliged to present themselves and half of them do not present themselves, at the Bureau des Constatations Médicales at Lourdes, and it is from this bureau's official reports that the list of cures is drawn up.

The estimate that about 4000 cures have been obtained at Lourdes within the first fifty years of the pilgrimage is undoubtedly considerably less than the actual number. The Bureau des Constatations stands near the shrine, and there are recorded and checked the certificates of maladies and also the certificates of cure; it is free to all physicians, whatever their nationality or religious belief. Consequently, on an average, from two to three hundred physicians annual visit this marvellous clinic.

As to the nature of the diseases which are cured, nervous disorders so frequently mentioned, do not furnish even the fourteenth part of the whole; 278 have been counted, out of a total of 3962. The present writer has published the number of cases of each disease or infirmity, among them tuberculosis, tumours, sores, cancers, deafness, blindness, etc. The "Annales des Sciences Physiques", a sceptical review whose chief editor is Doctor Ch. Richet, Professor at the Medical Faculty of Paris, said in the course of a long article, apropos of this faithful study: "On reading it, unprejudiced minds cannot but be convinced that the facts stated are authentic."

2) The Rosary

"The Rosary of the Virgin Mary, which gradually took form in the second millennium under the guidance of the Spirit of God, is a prayer loved by countless Saints and encouraged by the Magisterium. Simple yet profound, it still remains, at the dawn of this third millennium, a prayer of great significance, destined to bring forth a harvest of holiness. ...

The Rosary, though clearly Marian in character, is at heart a Christocentric prayer. In the sobriety of its elements, it has all the depth of the Gospel message in its entirety, of which it can be said to be a compendium. It is an echo of the prayer of Mary, her perennial Magnificat for the work of the redemptive Incarnation which began in her virginal womb. With the Rosary, the Christian people sits at the school of Mary and is led to contemplate the beauty on the face of Christ and to experience the depths of his love. Through the Rosary the faithful receive abundant grace, as though from the very hands of the Mother of the Redeemer."

Blessed Pope John Paul II
Rosarium Virginis Mariae Letter

"The Rosary is a Scripture-based prayer. It begins with the Apostles' Creed, which summarizes the great mysteries of the Catholic faith. The Our Father, which introduces each mystery, is from the Gospels. The first part of the Hail Mary is the angel's words announcing Christ's birth and Elizabeth's greeting to Mary. St. Pius V officially added the second part of the Hail Mary. The Mysteries of the Rosary center on the events of Christ's life. There are four sets of Mysteries: Joyful, Sorrowful, Glorious, and the Luminous. The repetition in the Rosary is meant to lead one into restful and contemplative prayer related to each Mystery. The gentle repetition of the words helps us to enter into the silence of our hearts, where Christ's spirit dwells."

United States Conference of
Catholic Bishops

3) *Praying the Rosary*

Pray the Beginning Rosary Prayers
    The Sign of the Cross
    The Apostles' Creed
    The Our Father
    Three Hail Mary's
    The Glory Be

Meditate & Pray the Five Mysteries for Today
    The Five Joyful Mysteries on Mondays & Saturdays
        Repeat this Prayer Decade for Each Mystery
            The Our Father
            Ten Hail Mary's
            The Glory Be
            O My Jesus
    The Five Sorrowful Mysteries on Tuesdays & Fridays
        Repeat this Prayer Decade for Each Mystery
            The Our Father
            Ten Hail Mary's
            The Glory Be
            O My Jesus
    The Five Glorious Mysteries on Wednesdays & Sundays
        Repeat this Prayer Decade for Each Mystery
            The Our Father
            Ten Hail Mary's
            The Glory Be
            O My Jesus
    The Five Luminous Mysteries on Thursdays
        Repeat this Prayer Decade for Each Mystery
            The Our Father
            Ten Hail Mary's
            The Glory Be
            O My Jesus

Pray the Ending Rosary Prayers
    Hail Holy Queen
    The Sign of the Cross

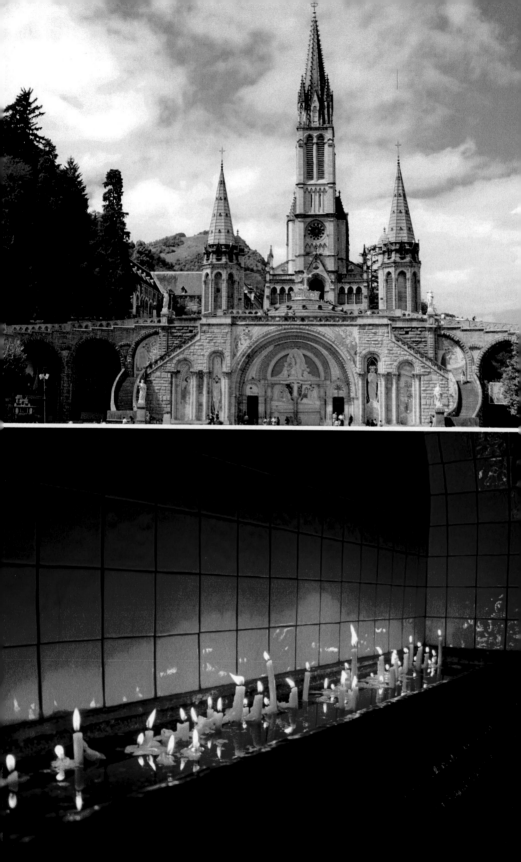

4) Beginning Rosary Prayers

In the name of the Father, and of the Son, and of the Holy Spirit. Amen.

I believe in God, the Father almighty, Creator of heaven and earth.
and in Jesus Christ, his only Son, Our Lord,
who was conceived by the Holy Spirit, born of the Virgin Mary,
suffered under Pontius Pilate, was crucified, died and was buried;
he descended into hell;
on the third day he rose again from the dead;
he ascended into heaven,
and is seated at the right hand of God the Father almighty;
from there he will come to judge the living and the dead.
I believe in the Holy Spirit, the holy catholic Church,
the communion of saints, the forgiveness of sins,
the resurrection of the body, and life everlasting.
Amen.

Our Father, who art in heaven, hallowed be thy name;
thy kingdom come; thy will be done on earth as it is in heaven.
Give us this day our daily bread; and forgive us our trespasses
as we forgive those who trespass against us;
and lead us not into temptation, but deliver us from evil.
Amen.

1) Hail Mary, full of grace, the Lord is with you! Blessed are you among women, and blessed is the fruit of thy womb, Jesus. Holy Mary, Mother of God, pray for us sinners, now and at the hour of our death. Amen.
2) Hail Mary, full of grace, the Lord is with you! Blessed are you among women, and blessed is the fruit of thy womb, Jesus. Holy Mary, Mother of God, pray for us sinners, now and at the hour of our death. Amen.
3) Hail Mary, full of grace, the Lord is with you! Blessed are you among women, and blessed is the fruit of thy womb, Jesus. Holy Mary, Mother of God, pray for us sinners, now and at the hour of our death. Amen.

Glory be to the Father, and to the Son, and to the Holy Spirit.
As it was in the beginning is now and ever shall be
world without end.
Amen

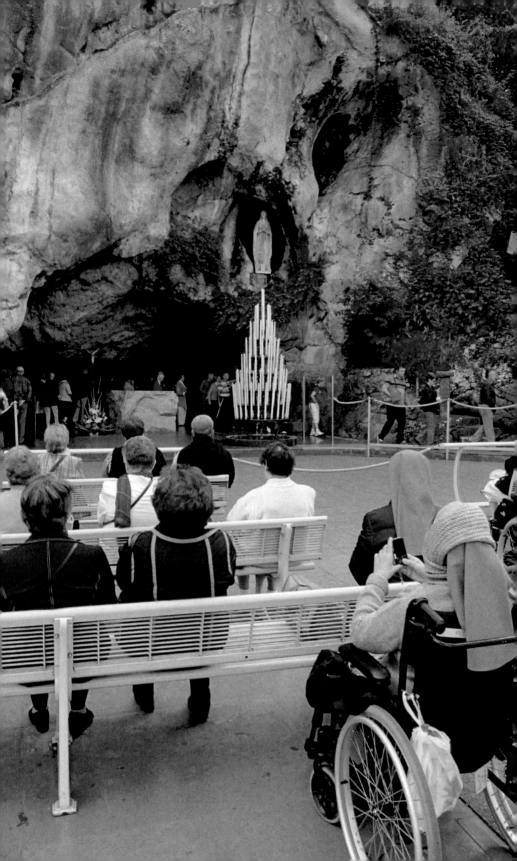

5) The Five Joyful Mysteries on Mondays & Saturdays

1st Joyful Mystery - The Annunciation
Luke 1:24-38

[24] After these days his wife Elizabeth conceived, and for five months she hid herself, saying, [25] "Thus the Lord has done to me in the days when he looked on me, to take away my reproach among men."

[26] In the sixth month the angel Gabriel was sent from God to a city of Galilee named Nazareth, [27] to a virgin betrothed to a man whose name was Joseph, of the house of David; and the virgin's name was Mary. [28] And he came to her and said, "Hail, full of grace, the Lord is with you!" [29] But she was greatly troubled at the saying, and considered in her mind what sort of greeting this might be. [30] And the angel said to her, "Do not be afraid, Mary, for you have found favor with God. [31] And behold, you will conceive in your womb and bear a son, and you shall call his name Jesus. [32] He will be great, and will be called the Son of the Most High; and the Lord God will give to him the throne of his father David, [33] and he will reign over the house of Jacob for ever; and of his kingdom there will be no end." [34] And Mary said to the angel, "How shall this be, since I have no husband?" [35] And the angel said to her,

"The Holy Spirit will come upon you, and the power of the Most High will overshadow you; therefore the child to be born will be called holy, the Son of God.

[36] And behold, your kinswoman Elizabeth in her old age has also conceived a son; and this is the sixth month with her who was called barren. [37] For with God nothing will be impossible." [38] And Mary said, "Behold, I am the handmaid of the Lord; let it be to me according to your word." And the angel departed from her.

Our Father, who art in heaven, hallowed be thy name;
thy kingdom come; thy will be done on earth as it is in heaven.
Give us this day our daily bread; and forgive us our trespasses
as we forgive those who trespass against us;
and lead us not into temptation, but deliver us from evil. Amen.

1) Hail Mary, full of grace, the Lord is with you! Blessed are you among women, and blessed is the fruit of thy womb, Jesus. Holy Mary, Mother of God, pray for us sinners, now and at the hour of our death. Amen.
2) Hail Mary, full of grace, the Lord is with you! Blessed are you among women, and blessed is the fruit of thy womb, Jesus. Holy Mary, Mother of God, pray for us sinners, now and at the hour of our death. Amen.
3) Hail Mary, full of grace, the Lord is with you! Blessed are you among women, and blessed is the fruit of thy womb, Jesus. Holy Mary, Mother of God, pray for us sinners, now and at the hour of our death. Amen.
4) Hail Mary, full of grace, the Lord is with you! Blessed are you among women, and blessed is the fruit of thy womb, Jesus. Holy Mary, Mother of God, pray for us sinners, now and at the hour of our death. Amen.
5) Hail Mary, full of grace, the Lord is with you! Blessed are you among women, and blessed is the fruit of thy womb, Jesus. Holy Mary, Mother of God, pray for us sinners, now and at the hour of our death. Amen.

6) Hail Mary, full of grace, the Lord is with you! Blessed are you among women, and blessed is the fruit of thy womb, Jesus. Holy Mary, Mother of God, pray for us sinners, now and at the hour of our death. Amen.
7) Hail Mary, full of grace, the Lord is with you! Blessed are you among women, and blessed is the fruit of thy womb, Jesus. Holy Mary, Mother of God, pray for us sinners, now and at the hour of our death. Amen.
8) Hail Mary, full of grace, the Lord is with you! Blessed are you among women, and blessed is the fruit of thy womb, Jesus. Holy Mary, Mother of God, pray for us sinners, now and at the hour of our death. Amen.
9) Hail Mary, full of grace, the Lord is with you! Blessed are you among women, and blessed is the fruit of thy womb, Jesus. Holy Mary, Mother of God, pray for us sinners, now and at the hour of our death. Amen.
10Hail Mary, full of grace, the Lord is with you! Blessed are you among women, and blessed is the fruit of thy womb, Jesus. Holy Mary, Mother of God, pray for us sinners, now and at the hour of our death. Amen.

Glory be to the Father, and to the Son, and to the Holy Spirit. As it was in the beginning is now and ever shall be world without end. Amen
O my Jesus, forgive us our sins, save us from the fire of Hell, lead all souls to Heaven, especially those who are in most need of your mercy.

2nd Joyful Mystery - The Visitation
Luke 1:39-56

[39] In those days Mary arose and went with haste into the hill country, to a city of Judah, [40] and she entered the house of Zechariah and greeted Elizabeth. [41] And when Elizabeth heard the greeting of Mary, the babe leaped in her womb; and Elizabeth was filled with the Holy Spirit [42] and she exclaimed with a loud cry, "Blessed are you among women, and blessed is the fruit of your womb! [43] And why is this granted me, that the mother of my Lord should come to me? [44] For behold, when the voice of your greeting came to my ears, the babe in my womb leaped for joy. [45] And blessed is she who believed that there would be a fulfilment of what was spoken to her from the Lord." [46] And Mary said,

"My soul magnifies the Lord, [47] and my spirit rejoices in God my Savior, [48] for he has regarded the low estate of his handmaiden. For behold, henceforth all generations will call me blessed; [49] for he who is mighty has done great things for me, and holy is his name. [50] And his mercy is on those who fear him from generation to generation. [51] He has shown strength with his arm, he has scattered the proud in the imagination of their hearts, [52] he has put down the mighty from their thrones, and exalted those of low degree; [53] he has filled the hungry with good things, and the rich he has sent empty away. [54] He has helped his servant Israel, in remembrance of his mercy, [55] as he spoke to our fathers, to Abraham and to his posterity for ever." [56] And Mary remained with her about three months, and returned to her home.

Our Father, who art in heaven, hallowed be thy name;
thy kingdom come; thy will be done on earth as it is in heaven.
Give us this day our daily bread; and forgive us our trespasses
as we forgive those who trespass against us;
and lead us not into temptation, but deliver us from evil. Amen.

1) Hail Mary, full of grace, the Lord is with you! Blessed are you among women, and blessed is the fruit of thy womb, Jesus. Holy Mary, Mother of God, pray for us sinners, now and at the hour of our death. Amen.
2) Hail Mary, full of grace, the Lord is with you! Blessed are you among women, and blessed is the fruit of thy womb, Jesus. Holy Mary, Mother of God, pray for us sinners, now and at the hour of our death. Amen.
3) Hail Mary, full of grace, the Lord is with you! Blessed are you among women, and blessed is the fruit of thy womb, Jesus. Holy Mary, Mother of God, pray for us sinners, now and at the hour of our death. Amen.
4) Hail Mary, full of grace, the Lord is with you! Blessed are you among women, and blessed is the fruit of thy womb, Jesus. Holy Mary, Mother of God, pray for us sinners, now and at the hour of our death. Amen.
5) Hail Mary, full of grace, the Lord is with you! Blessed are you among women, and blessed is the fruit of thy womb, Jesus. Holy Mary, Mother of God, pray for us sinners, now and at the hour of our death. Amen.

6) Hail Mary, full of grace, the Lord is with you! Blessed are you among women, and blessed is the fruit of thy womb, Jesus. Holy Mary, Mother of God, pray for us sinners, now and at the hour of our death. Amen.
7) Hail Mary, full of grace, the Lord is with you! Blessed are you among women, and blessed is the fruit of thy womb, Jesus. Holy Mary, Mother of God, pray for us sinners, now and at the hour of our death. Amen.
8) Hail Mary, full of grace, the Lord is with you! Blessed are you among women, and blessed is the fruit of thy womb, Jesus. Holy Mary, Mother of God, pray for us sinners, now and at the hour of our death. Amen.
9) Hail Mary, full of grace, the Lord is with you! Blessed are you among women, and blessed is the fruit of thy womb, Jesus. Holy Mary, Mother of God, pray for us sinners, now and at the hour of our death. Amen.
10Hail Mary, full of grace, the Lord is with you! Blessed are you among women, and blessed is the fruit of thy womb, Jesus. Holy Mary, Mother of God, pray for us sinners, now and at the hour of our death. Amen.

Glory be to the Father, and to the Son, and to the Holy Spirit. As it was in the beginning is now and ever shall be world without end. Amen
O my Jesus, forgive us our sins, save us from the fire of Hell, lead all souls to Heaven, especially those who are in most need of your mercy.

3rd Joyful Mystery - The Nativity
Luke 2:1-20

[1] In those days a decree went out from Caesar Augustus that all the world should be enrolled. [2] This was the first enrollment, when Quirini-us was governor of Syria. [3] And all went to be enrolled, each to his own city. [4] And Joseph also went up from Galilee, from the city of Nazareth, to Judea, to the city of David, which is called Bethlehem, because he was of the house and lineage of David, [5] to be enrolled with Mary, his betrothed, who was with child. [6] And while they were there, the time came for her to be delivered. [7] And she gave birth to her first-born son and wrapped him in swaddling cloths, and laid him in a manger, because there was no place for them in the inn.

[8] And in that region there were shepherds out in the field, keeping watch over their flock by night. [9] And an angel of the Lord appeared to them, and the glory of the Lord shone around them, and they were filled with fear. [10] And the angel said to them, "Be not afraid; for behold, I bring you good news of a great joy which will come to all the people; [11] for to you is born this day in the city of David a Savior, who is Christ the Lord. [12] And this will be a sign for you: you will find a babe wrapped in swaddling cloths and lying in a manger." [13] And suddenly there was with the angel a multitude of the heavenly host praising God and saying, [14] "Glory to God in the highest, and on earth peace among men with whom he is pleased!"

[15] When the angels went away from them into heaven, the shepherds said to one another, "Let us go over to Bethlehem and see this thing that has happened, which the Lord has made known to us." [16] And they went with haste, and found Mary and Joseph, and the babe lying in a manger. [17] And when they saw it they made known the saying which had been told them concerning this child; [18] and all who heard it wondered at what the shepherds told them. [19] But Mary kept all these things, pondering them in her heart. [20] And the shepherds returned, glorifying and praising God for all they had heard and seen, as it had been told them.

Our Father, who art in heaven, hallowed be thy name;
thy kingdom come; thy will be done on earth as it is in heaven.
Give us this day our daily bread; and forgive us our trespasses
as we forgive those who trespass against us;
and lead us not into temptation, but deliver us from evil. Amen.

1) Hail Mary, full of grace, the Lord is with you! Blessed are you among women, and blessed is the fruit of thy womb, Jesus. Holy Mary, Mother of God, pray for us sinners, now and at the hour of our death. Amen.
2) Hail Mary, full of grace, the Lord is with you! Blessed are you among women, and blessed is the fruit of thy womb, Jesus. Holy Mary, Mother of God, pray for us sinners, now and at the hour of our death. Amen.
3) Hail Mary, full of grace, the Lord is with you! Blessed are you among women, and blessed is the fruit of thy womb, Jesus. Holy Mary, Mother of God, pray for us sinners, now and at the hour of our death. Amen.
4) Hail Mary, full of grace, the Lord is with you! Blessed are you among women, and blessed is the fruit of thy womb, Jesus. Holy Mary, Mother of God, pray for us sinners, now and at the hour of our death. Amen.
5) Hail Mary, full of grace, the Lord is with you! Blessed are you among women, and blessed is the fruit of thy womb, Jesus. Holy Mary, Mother of God, pray for us sinners, now and at the hour of our death. Amen.

6) Hail Mary, full of grace, the Lord is with you! Blessed are you among women, and blessed is the fruit of thy womb, Jesus. Holy Mary, Mother of God, pray for us sinners, now and at the hour of our death. Amen.
7) Hail Mary, full of grace, the Lord is with you! Blessed are you among women, and blessed is the fruit of thy womb, Jesus. Holy Mary, Mother of God, pray for us sinners, now and at the hour of our death. Amen.
8) Hail Mary, full of grace, the Lord is with you! Blessed are you among women, and blessed is the fruit of thy womb, Jesus. Holy Mary, Mother of God, pray for us sinners, now and at the hour of our death. Amen.
9) Hail Mary, full of grace, the Lord is with you! Blessed are you among women, and blessed is the fruit of thy womb, Jesus. Holy Mary, Mother of God, pray for us sinners, now and at the hour of our death. Amen.
10Hail Mary, full of grace, the Lord is with you! Blessed are you among women, and blessed is the fruit of thy womb, Jesus. Holy Mary, Mother of God, pray for us sinners, now and at the hour of our death. Amen.

Glory be to the Father, and to the Son, and to the Holy Spirit. As it was in the beginning is now and ever shall be world without end. Amen
O my Jesus, forgive us our sins, save us from the fire of Hell, lead all souls to Heaven, especially those who are in most need of your mercy.

4th Joyful Mystery - The Presentation in the Temple
Luke 2:22-40

[22] And when the time came for their purification according to the law of Moses, they brought him up to Jerusalem to present him to the Lord [23] (as it is written in the law of the Lord, "Every male that opens the womb shall be called holy to the Lord") [24] and to offer a sacrifice according to what is said in the law of the Lord, "a pair of turtledoves, or two young pigeons." [25] Now there was a man in Jerusalem, whose name was Simeon, and this man was righteous and devout, looking for the consolation of Israel, and the Holy Spirit was upon him. [26] And it had been revealed to him by the Holy Spirit that he should not see death before he had seen the Lord's Christ. [27] And inspired by the Spirit he came into the temple; and when the parents brought in the child Jesus, to do for him according to the custom of the law, [28] he took him up in his arms and blessed God and said, [29] "Lord, now lettest thou thy servant depart in peace, according to thy word; [30] for mine eyes have seen thy salvation [31] which thou hast prepared in the presence of all peoples, [32] a light for revelation to the Gentiles, and for glory to thy people Israel."

[33] And his father and his mother marveled at what was said about him; [34] and Simeon blessed them and said to Mary his mother, "Behold, this child is set for the fall and rising of many in Israel, and for a sign that is spoken against [35] (and a sword will pierce through your own soul also), that thoughts out of many hearts may be revealed."

[36] And there was a prophetess, Anna, the daughter of Phanu-el, of the tribe of Asher; she was of a great age, having lived with her husband seven years from her virginity, [37] and as a widow till she was eighty-four. She did not depart from the temple, worshiping with fasting and prayer night and day. [38] And coming up at that very hour she gave thanks to God, and spoke of him to all who were looking for the redemption of Jerusalem.

[39] And when they had performed everything according to the law of the Lord, they returned into Galilee, to their own city, Nazareth. [40] And the child grew and became strong, filled with wisdom; and the favor of God was upon him.

Our Father, who art in heaven, hallowed be thy name;
thy kingdom come; thy will be done on earth as it is in heaven.
Give us this day our daily bread; and forgive us our trespasses
as we forgive those who trespass against us;
and lead us not into temptation, but deliver us from evil. Amen.

1) Hail Mary, full of grace, the Lord is with you! Blessed are you among
women, and blessed is the fruit of thy womb, Jesus. Holy Mary, Mother
of God, pray for us sinners, now and at the hour of our death. Amen.
2) Hail Mary, full of grace, the Lord is with you! Blessed are you among
women, and blessed is the fruit of thy womb, Jesus. Holy Mary, Mother
of God, pray for us sinners, now and at the hour of our death. Amen.
3) Hail Mary, full of grace, the Lord is with you! Blessed are you among
women, and blessed is the fruit of thy womb, Jesus. Holy Mary, Mother
of God, pray for us sinners, now and at the hour of our death. Amen.
4) Hail Mary, full of grace, the Lord is with you! Blessed are you among
women, and blessed is the fruit of thy womb, Jesus. Holy Mary, Mother
of God, pray for us sinners, now and at the hour of our death. Amen.
5) Hail Mary, full of grace, the Lord is with you! Blessed are you among
women, and blessed is the fruit of thy womb, Jesus. Holy Mary, Mother
of God, pray for us sinners, now and at the hour of our death. Amen.

6) Hail Mary, full of grace, the Lord is with you! Blessed are you among
women, and blessed is the fruit of thy womb, Jesus. Holy Mary, Mother
of God, pray for us sinners, now and at the hour of our death. Amen.
7) Hail Mary, full of grace, the Lord is with you! Blessed are you among
women, and blessed is the fruit of thy womb, Jesus. Holy Mary, Mother
of God, pray for us sinners, now and at the hour of our death. Amen.
8) Hail Mary, full of grace, the Lord is with you! Blessed are you among
women, and blessed is the fruit of thy womb, Jesus. Holy Mary, Mother
of God, pray for us sinners, now and at the hour of our death. Amen.
9) Hail Mary, full of grace, the Lord is with you! Blessed are you among
women, and blessed is the fruit of thy womb, Jesus. Holy Mary, Mother
of God, pray for us sinners, now and at the hour of our death. Amen.
10Hail Mary, full of grace, the Lord is with you! Blessed are you among
women, and blessed is the fruit of thy womb, Jesus. Holy Mary, Mother
of God, pray for us sinners, now and at the hour of our death. Amen.

Glory be to the Father, and to the Son, and to the Holy Spirit. As it was
in the beginning is now and ever shall be world without end. Amen
O my Jesus, forgive us our sins, save us from the fire of Hell, lead all
souls to Heaven, especially those who are in most need of your mercy.

5th Joyful Mystery - The Finding in the Temple
Luke 2:41-52

[41] Now his parents went to Jerusalem every year at the feast of the Passover. [42] And when he was twelve years old, they went up according to custom; [43] and when the feast was ended, as they were returning, the boy Jesus stayed behind in Jerusalem. His parents did not know it, [44] but supposing him to be in the company they went a day's journey, and they sought him among their kinsfolk and acquaintances; [45] and when they did not find him, they returned to Jerusalem, seeking him. [46] After three days they found him in the temple, sitting among the teachers, listening to them and asking them questions; [47] and all who heard him were amazed at his understanding and his answers. [48] And when they saw him they were astonished; and his mother said to him, "Son, why have you treated us so? Behold, your father and I have been looking for you anxiously." [49] And he said to them, "How is it that you sought me? Did you not know that I must be in my Father's house?" [50] And they did not understand the saying which he spoke to them. [51] And he went down with them and came to Nazareth, and was obedient to them; and his mother kept all these things in her heart.

[52] And Jesus increased in wisdom and in stature, and in favor with God and man.

Our Father, who art in heaven, hallowed be thy name;
thy kingdom come; thy will be done on earth as it is in heaven.
Give us this day our daily bread; and forgive us our trespasses
as we forgive those who trespass against us;
and lead us not into temptation, but deliver us from evil. Amen.

1) Hail Mary, full of grace, the Lord is with you! Blessed are you among women, and blessed is the fruit of thy womb, Jesus. Holy Mary, Mother of God, pray for us sinners, now and at the hour of our death. Amen.
2) Hail Mary, full of grace, the Lord is with you! Blessed are you among women, and blessed is the fruit of thy womb, Jesus. Holy Mary, Mother of God, pray for us sinners, now and at the hour of our death. Amen.
3) Hail Mary, full of grace, the Lord is with you! Blessed are you among women, and blessed is the fruit of thy womb, Jesus. Holy Mary, Mother of God, pray for us sinners, now and at the hour of our death. Amen.
4) Hail Mary, full of grace, the Lord is with you! Blessed are you among women, and blessed is the fruit of thy womb, Jesus. Holy Mary, Mother of God, pray for us sinners, now and at the hour of our death. Amen.
5) Hail Mary, full of grace, the Lord is with you! Blessed are you among women, and blessed is the fruit of thy womb, Jesus. Holy Mary, Mother of God, pray for us sinners, now and at the hour of our death. Amen.

6) Hail Mary, full of grace, the Lord is with you! Blessed are you among women, and blessed is the fruit of thy womb, Jesus. Holy Mary, Mother of God, pray for us sinners, now and at the hour of our death. Amen.
7) Hail Mary, full of grace, the Lord is with you! Blessed are you among women, and blessed is the fruit of thy womb, Jesus. Holy Mary, Mother of God, pray for us sinners, now and at the hour of our death. Amen.
8) Hail Mary, full of grace, the Lord is with you! Blessed are you among women, and blessed is the fruit of thy womb, Jesus. Holy Mary, Mother of God, pray for us sinners, now and at the hour of our death. Amen.
9) Hail Mary, full of grace, the Lord is with you! Blessed are you among women, and blessed is the fruit of thy womb, Jesus. Holy Mary, Mother of God, pray for us sinners, now and at the hour of our death. Amen.
10Hail Mary, full of grace, the Lord is with you! Blessed are you among women, and blessed is the fruit of thy womb, Jesus. Holy Mary, Mother of God, pray for us sinners, now and at the hour of our death. Amen.

Glory be to the Father, and to the Son, and to the Holy Spirit. As it was in the beginning is now and ever shall be world without end. Amen
O my Jesus, forgive us our sins, save us from the fire of Hell, lead all souls to Heaven, especially those who are in most need of your mercy.

6) The Five Sorrowful Mysteries on Tuesdays & Fridays

1st Sorrowful Mystery - The Agony in the Garden
Matthew 27:36-50

[36] Then Jesus went with them to a place called Gethsemane, and he said to his disciples, "Sit here, while I go yonder and pray." [37] And taking with him Peter and the two sons of Zebedee, he began to be sorrowful and troubled. [38] Then he said to them, "My soul is very sorrowful, even to death; remain here, and watch with me." [39] And going a little farther he fell on his face and prayed, "My Father, if it be possible, let this cup pass from me; nevertheless, not as I will, but as thou wilt." [40] And he came to the disciples and found them sleeping; and he said to Peter, "So, could you not watch with me one hour? [41] Watch and pray that you may not enter into temptation; the spirit indeed is willing, but the flesh is weak." [42] Again, for the second time, he went away and prayed, "My Father, if this cannot pass unless I drink it, thy will be done." [43] And again he came and found them sleeping, for their eyes were heavy. [44] So, leaving them again, he went away and prayed for the third time, saying the same words. [45] Then he came to the disciples and said to them, "Are you still sleeping and taking your rest? Behold, the hour is at hand, and the Son of man is betrayed into the hands of sinners. [46] Rise, let us be going; see, my betrayer is at hand."

[47] While he was still speaking, Judas came, one of the twelve, and with him a great crowd with swords and clubs, from the chief priests and the elders of the people. [48] Now the betrayer had given them a sign, saying, "The one I shall kiss is the man; seize him." [49] And he came up to Jesus at once and said, "Hail, Master!" And he kissed him. [50] Jesus said to him, "Friend, why are you here?" Then they came up and laid hands on Jesus and seized him.

Our Father, who art in heaven, hallowed be thy name; thy kingdom come; thy will be done on earth as it is in heaven. Give us this day our daily bread; and forgive us our trespasses as we forgive those who trespass against us; and lead us not into temptation, but deliver us from evil. Amen.

1) Hail Mary, full of grace, the Lord is with you! Blessed are you among women, and blessed is the fruit of thy womb, Jesus. Holy Mary, Mother of God, pray for us sinners, now and at the hour of our death. Amen.
2) Hail Mary, full of grace, the Lord is with you! Blessed are you among women, and blessed is the fruit of thy womb, Jesus. Holy Mary, Mother of God, pray for us sinners, now and at the hour of our death. Amen.
3) Hail Mary, full of grace, the Lord is with you! Blessed are you among women, and blessed is the fruit of thy womb, Jesus. Holy Mary, Mother of God, pray for us sinners, now and at the hour of our death. Amen.
4) Hail Mary, full of grace, the Lord is with you! Blessed are you among women, and blessed is the fruit of thy womb, Jesus. Holy Mary, Mother of God, pray for us sinners, now and at the hour of our death. Amen.
5) Hail Mary, full of grace, the Lord is with you! Blessed are you among women, and blessed is the fruit of thy womb, Jesus. Holy Mary, Mother of God, pray for us sinners, now and at the hour of our death. Amen.

6) Hail Mary, full of grace, the Lord is with you! Blessed are you among women, and blessed is the fruit of thy womb, Jesus. Holy Mary, Mother of God, pray for us sinners, now and at the hour of our death. Amen.
7) Hail Mary, full of grace, the Lord is with you! Blessed are you among women, and blessed is the fruit of thy womb, Jesus. Holy Mary, Mother of God, pray for us sinners, now and at the hour of our death. Amen.
8) Hail Mary, full of grace, the Lord is with you! Blessed are you among women, and blessed is the fruit of thy womb, Jesus. Holy Mary, Mother of God, pray for us sinners, now and at the hour of our death. Amen.
9) Hail Mary, full of grace, the Lord is with you! Blessed are you among women, and blessed is the fruit of thy womb, Jesus. Holy Mary, Mother of God, pray for us sinners, now and at the hour of our death. Amen.
10Hail Mary, full of grace, the Lord is with you! Blessed are you among women, and blessed is the fruit of thy womb, Jesus. Holy Mary, Mother of God, pray for us sinners, now and at the hour of our death. Amen.

Glory be to the Father, and to the Son, and to the Holy Spirit. As it was in the beginning is now and ever shall be world without end. Amen
O my Jesus, forgive us our sins, save us from the fire of Hell, lead all souls to Heaven, especially those who are in most need of your mercy.

2nd Sorrowful Mystery - The Scourging at the Pillar
Matthew 27:24-26

[24] So when Pilate saw that he was gaining nothing, but rather that a riot was beginning, he took water and washed his hands before the crowd, saying, "I am innocent of this righteous man's blood; see to it yourselves." [25] And all the people answered, "His blood be on us and on our children!" [26] Then he released for them Barabbas, and having scourged Jesus, delivered him to be crucified.

Our Father, who art in heaven, hallowed be thy name;
thy kingdom come; thy will be done on earth as it is in heaven.
Give us this day our daily bread; and forgive us our trespasses
as we forgive those who trespass against us;
and lead us not into temptation, but deliver us from evil. Amen.

1) Hail Mary, full of grace, the Lord is with you! Blessed are you among women, and blessed is the fruit of thy womb, Jesus. Holy Mary, Mother of God, pray for us sinners, now and at the hour of our death. Amen.
2) Hail Mary, full of grace, the Lord is with you! Blessed are you among women, and blessed is the fruit of thy womb, Jesus. Holy Mary, Mother of God, pray for us sinners, now and at the hour of our death. Amen.
3) Hail Mary, full of grace, the Lord is with you! Blessed are you among women, and blessed is the fruit of thy womb, Jesus. Holy Mary, Mother of God, pray for us sinners, now and at the hour of our death. Amen.
4) Hail Mary, full of grace, the Lord is with you! Blessed are you among women, and blessed is the fruit of thy womb, Jesus. Holy Mary, Mother of God, pray for us sinners, now and at the hour of our death. Amen.
5) Hail Mary, full of grace, the Lord is with you! Blessed are you among women, and blessed is the fruit of thy womb, Jesus. Holy Mary, Mother of God, pray for us sinners, now and at the hour of our death. Amen.

6) Hail Mary, full of grace, the Lord is with you! Blessed are you among women, and blessed is the fruit of thy womb, Jesus. Holy Mary, Mother of God, pray for us sinners, now and at the hour of our death. Amen.
7) Hail Mary, full of grace, the Lord is with you! Blessed are you among women, and blessed is the fruit of thy womb, Jesus. Holy Mary, Mother of God, pray for us sinners, now and at the hour of our death. Amen.
8) Hail Mary, full of grace, the Lord is with you! Blessed are you among women, and blessed is the fruit of thy womb, Jesus. Holy Mary, Mother of God, pray for us sinners, now and at the hour of our death. Amen.
9) Hail Mary, full of grace, the Lord is with you! Blessed are you among women, and blessed is the fruit of thy womb, Jesus. Holy Mary, Mother of God, pray for us sinners, now and at the hour of our death. Amen.
10 Hail Mary, full of grace, the Lord is with you! Blessed are you among women, and blessed is the fruit of thy womb, Jesus. Holy Mary, Mother of God, pray for us sinners, now and at the hour of our death. Amen.

Glory be to the Father, and to the Son, and to the Holy Spirit. As it was in the beginning is now and ever shall be world without end. Amen
O my Jesus, forgive us our sins, save us from the fire of Hell, lead all souls to Heaven, especially those who are in most need of your mercy.

3rd Sorrowful Mystery - The Crowning with Thorns
Matthew 27:27-31

[27] Then the soldiers of the governor took Jesus into the praetorium, and they gathered the whole battalion before him. [28] And they stripped him and put a scarlet robe upon him, [29] and plaiting a crown of thorns they put it on his head, and put a reed in his right hand. And kneeling before him they mocked him, saying, "Hail, King of the Jews!" [30] And they spat upon him, and took the reed and struck him on the head. [31] And when they had mocked him, they stripped him of the robe, and put his own clothes on him, and led him away to crucify him.

Our Father, who art in heaven, hallowed be thy name;
thy kingdom come; thy will be done on earth as it is in heaven.
Give us this day our daily bread; and forgive us our trespasses
as we forgive those who trespass against us;
and lead us not into temptation, but deliver us from evil. Amen.

1) Hail Mary, full of grace, the Lord is with you! Blessed are you among women, and blessed is the fruit of thy womb, Jesus. Holy Mary, Mother of God, pray for us sinners, now and at the hour of our death. Amen.
2) Hail Mary, full of grace, the Lord is with you! Blessed are you among women, and blessed is the fruit of thy womb, Jesus. Holy Mary, Mother of God, pray for us sinners, now and at the hour of our death. Amen.
3) Hail Mary, full of grace, the Lord is with you! Blessed are you among women, and blessed is the fruit of thy womb, Jesus. Holy Mary, Mother of God, pray for us sinners, now and at the hour of our death. Amen.
4) Hail Mary, full of grace, the Lord is with you! Blessed are you among women, and blessed is the fruit of thy womb, Jesus. Holy Mary, Mother of God, pray for us sinners, now and at the hour of our death. Amen.
5) Hail Mary, full of grace, the Lord is with you! Blessed are you among women, and blessed is the fruit of thy womb, Jesus. Holy Mary, Mother of God, pray for us sinners, now and at the hour of our death. Amen.

6) Hail Mary, full of grace, the Lord is with you! Blessed are you among women, and blessed is the fruit of thy womb, Jesus. Holy Mary, Mother of God, pray for us sinners, now and at the hour of our death. Amen.
7) Hail Mary, full of grace, the Lord is with you! Blessed are you among women, and blessed is the fruit of thy womb, Jesus. Holy Mary, Mother of God, pray for us sinners, now and at the hour of our death. Amen.
8) Hail Mary, full of grace, the Lord is with you! Blessed are you among women, and blessed is the fruit of thy womb, Jesus. Holy Mary, Mother of God, pray for us sinners, now and at the hour of our death. Amen.
9) Hail Mary, full of grace, the Lord is with you! Blessed are you among women, and blessed is the fruit of thy womb, Jesus. Holy Mary, Mother of God, pray for us sinners, now and at the hour of our death. Amen.
10Hail Mary, full of grace, the Lord is with you! Blessed are you among women, and blessed is the fruit of thy womb, Jesus. Holy Mary, Mother of God, pray for us sinners, now and at the hour of our death. Amen.

Glory be to the Father, and to the Son, and to the Holy Spirit. As it was in the beginning is now and ever shall be world without end. Amen
O my Jesus, forgive us our sins, save us from the fire of Hell, lead all souls to Heaven, especially those who are in most need of your mercy.

4th Sorrowful Mystery - The Carrying of the Cross
John 19:12-17

[12] Upon this Pilate sought to release him, but the Jews cried out, "If you release this man, you are not Caesar's friend; every one who makes himself a king sets himself against Caesar." [13] When Pilate heard these words, he brought Jesus out and sat down on the judgment seat at a place called The Pavement, and in Hebrew, Gabbatha. [14] Now it was the day of Preparation of the Passover; it was about the sixth hour. He said to the Jews, "Behold your King!" [15] They cried out, "Away with him, away with him, crucify him!" Pilate said to them, "Shall I crucify your King?" The chief priests answered, "We have no king but Caesar." [16] Then he handed him over to them to be crucified.

[17] So they took Jesus, and he went out, bearing his own cross, to the place called the place of a skull, which is called in Hebrew Golgotha.

Our Father, who art in heaven, hallowed be thy name;
thy kingdom come; thy will be done on earth as it is in heaven.
Give us this day our daily bread; and forgive us our trespasses
as we forgive those who trespass against us;
and lead us not into temptation, but deliver us from evil. Amen.

1) Hail Mary, full of grace, the Lord is with you! Blessed are you among
women, and blessed is the fruit of thy womb, Jesus. Holy Mary, Mother
of God, pray for us sinners, now and at the hour of our death. Amen.
2) Hail Mary, full of grace, the Lord is with you! Blessed are you among
women, and blessed is the fruit of thy womb, Jesus. Holy Mary, Mother
of God, pray for us sinners, now and at the hour of our death. Amen.
3) Hail Mary, full of grace, the Lord is with you! Blessed are you among
women, and blessed is the fruit of thy womb, Jesus. Holy Mary, Mother
of God, pray for us sinners, now and at the hour of our death. Amen.
4) Hail Mary, full of grace, the Lord is with you! Blessed are you among
women, and blessed is the fruit of thy womb, Jesus. Holy Mary, Mother
of God, pray for us sinners, now and at the hour of our death. Amen.
5) Hail Mary, full of grace, the Lord is with you! Blessed are you among
women, and blessed is the fruit of thy womb, Jesus. Holy Mary, Mother
of God, pray for us sinners, now and at the hour of our death. Amen.

6) Hail Mary, full of grace, the Lord is with you! Blessed are you among
women, and blessed is the fruit of thy womb, Jesus. Holy Mary, Mother
of God, pray for us sinners, now and at the hour of our death. Amen.
7) Hail Mary, full of grace, the Lord is with you! Blessed are you among
women, and blessed is the fruit of thy womb, Jesus. Holy Mary, Mother
of God, pray for us sinners, now and at the hour of our death. Amen.
8) Hail Mary, full of grace, the Lord is with you! Blessed are you among
women, and blessed is the fruit of thy womb, Jesus. Holy Mary, Mother
of God, pray for us sinners, now and at the hour of our death. Amen.
9) Hail Mary, full of grace, the Lord is with you! Blessed are you among
women, and blessed is the fruit of thy womb, Jesus. Holy Mary, Mother
of God, pray for us sinners, now and at the hour of our death. Amen.
10Hail Mary, full of grace, the Lord is with you! Blessed are you among
women, and blessed is the fruit of thy womb, Jesus. Holy Mary, Mother
of God, pray for us sinners, now and at the hour of our death. Amen.

Glory be to the Father, and to the Son, and to the Holy Spirit. As it was
in the beginning is now and ever shall be world without end. Amen
O my Jesus, forgive us our sins, save us from the fire of Hell, lead all
souls to Heaven, especially those who are in most need of your mercy.

5th Sorrowful Mystery - The Crucifixion and Death
John 19:18-30

[18] There they crucified him, and with him two others, one on either side, and Jesus between them. [19] Pilate also wrote a title and put it on the cross; it read, "Jesus of Nazareth, the King of the Jews." [20] Many of the Jews read this title, for the place where Jesus was crucified was near the city; and it was written in Hebrew, in Latin, and in Greek. [21] The chief priests of the Jews then said to Pilate, "Do not write, 'The King of the Jews,' but, 'This man said, I am King of the Jews.'" [22] Pilate answered, "What I have written I have written."

[23] When the soldiers had crucified Jesus they took his garments and made four parts, one for each soldier; also his tunic. But the tunic was without seam, woven from top to bottom; [24] so they said to one another, "Let us not tear it, but cast lots for it to see whose it shall be." This was to fulfil the scripture, "They parted my garments among them, and for my clothing they cast lots."

[25] So the soldiers did this. But standing by the cross of Jesus were his mother, and his mother's sister, Mary the wife of Clopas, and Mary Magdalene. [26] When Jesus saw his mother, and the disciple whom he loved standing near, he said to his mother, "Woman, behold, your son!" [27] Then he said to the disciple, "Behold, your mother!" And from that hour the disciple took her to his own home.

[28] After this Jesus, knowing that all was now finished, said (to fulfill the scripture), "I thirst." [29] A bowl full of vinegar stood there; so they put a sponge full of the vinegar on hyssop and held it to his mouth. [30] When Jesus had received the vinegar, he said, "It is finished"; and he bowed his head and gave up his spirit.

Our Father, who art in heaven, hallowed be thy name;
thy kingdom come; thy will be done on earth as it is in heaven.
Give us this day our daily bread; and forgive us our trespasses
as we forgive those who trespass against us;
and lead us not into temptation, but deliver us from evil. Amen.

1) Hail Mary, full of grace, the Lord is with you! Blessed are you among women, and blessed is the fruit of thy womb, Jesus. Holy Mary, Mother of God, pray for us sinners, now and at the hour of our death. Amen.
2) Hail Mary, full of grace, the Lord is with you! Blessed are you among women, and blessed is the fruit of thy womb, Jesus. Holy Mary, Mother of God, pray for us sinners, now and at the hour of our death. Amen.
3) Hail Mary, full of grace, the Lord is with you! Blessed are you among women, and blessed is the fruit of thy womb, Jesus. Holy Mary, Mother of God, pray for us sinners, now and at the hour of our death. Amen.
4) Hail Mary, full of grace, the Lord is with you! Blessed are you among women, and blessed is the fruit of thy womb, Jesus. Holy Mary, Mother of God, pray for us sinners, now and at the hour of our death. Amen.
5) Hail Mary, full of grace, the Lord is with you! Blessed are you among women, and blessed is the fruit of thy womb, Jesus. Holy Mary, Mother of God, pray for us sinners, now and at the hour of our death. Amen.

6) Hail Mary, full of grace, the Lord is with you! Blessed are you among women, and blessed is the fruit of thy womb, Jesus. Holy Mary, Mother of God, pray for us sinners, now and at the hour of our death. Amen.
7) Hail Mary, full of grace, the Lord is with you! Blessed are you among women, and blessed is the fruit of thy womb, Jesus. Holy Mary, Mother of God, pray for us sinners, now and at the hour of our death. Amen.
8) Hail Mary, full of grace, the Lord is with you! Blessed are you among women, and blessed is the fruit of thy womb, Jesus. Holy Mary, Mother of God, pray for us sinners, now and at the hour of our death. Amen.
9) Hail Mary, full of grace, the Lord is with you! Blessed are you among women, and blessed is the fruit of thy womb, Jesus. Holy Mary, Mother of God, pray for us sinners, now and at the hour of our death. Amen.
10Hail Mary, full of grace, the Lord is with you! Blessed are you among women, and blessed is the fruit of thy womb, Jesus. Holy Mary, Mother of God, pray for us sinners, now and at the hour of our death. Amen.

Glory be to the Father, and to the Son, and to the Holy Spirit. As it was in the beginning is now and ever shall be world without end. Amen
O my Jesus, forgive us our sins, save us from the fire of Hell, lead all souls to Heaven, especially those who are in most need of your mercy.

7) The Five Glorious Mysteries on Wednesdays & Sundays

1st Glorious Mystery - The Resurrection
Luke 24:1-12

[1] But on the first day of the week, at early dawn, they went to the tomb, taking the spices which they had prepared. [2] And they found the stone rolled away from the tomb, [3] but when they went in they did not find the body. [4] While they were perplexed about this, behold, two men stood by them in dazzling apparel; [5] and as they were frightened and bowed their faces to the ground, the men said to them, "Why do you seek the living among the dead? He is not here, but has risen. [6] Remember how he told you, while he was still in Galilee, [7] that the Son of man must be delivered into the hands of sinful men, and be crucified, and on the third day rise." [8] And they remembered his words, [9] and returning from the tomb they told all this to the eleven and to all the rest. [10] Now it was Mary Magdalene and Jo-anna and Mary the mother of James and the other women with them who told this to the apostles; [11] but these words seemed to them an idle tale, and they did not believe them. [12] But Peter rose and ran to the tomb; stooping and looking in, he saw the linen cloths by themselves; and he went home wondering at what had happened.

Our Father, who art in heaven, hallowed be thy name;
thy kingdom come; thy will be done on earth as it is in heaven.
Give us this day our daily bread; and forgive us our trespasses
as we forgive those who trespass against us;
and lead us not into temptation, but deliver us from evil. Amen.

1) Hail Mary, full of grace, the Lord is with you! Blessed are you among
women, and blessed is the fruit of thy womb, Jesus. Holy Mary, Mother
of God, pray for us sinners, now and at the hour of our death. Amen.
2) Hail Mary, full of grace, the Lord is with you! Blessed are you among
women, and blessed is the fruit of thy womb, Jesus. Holy Mary, Mother
of God, pray for us sinners, now and at the hour of our death. Amen.
3) Hail Mary, full of grace, the Lord is with you! Blessed are you among
women, and blessed is the fruit of thy womb, Jesus. Holy Mary, Mother
of God, pray for us sinners, now and at the hour of our death. Amen.
4) Hail Mary, full of grace, the Lord is with you! Blessed are you among
women, and blessed is the fruit of thy womb, Jesus. Holy Mary, Mother
of God, pray for us sinners, now and at the hour of our death. Amen.
5) Hail Mary, full of grace, the Lord is with you! Blessed are you among
women, and blessed is the fruit of thy womb, Jesus. Holy Mary, Mother
of God, pray for us sinners, now and at the hour of our death. Amen.

6) Hail Mary, full of grace, the Lord is with you! Blessed are you among
women, and blessed is the fruit of thy womb, Jesus. Holy Mary, Mother
of God, pray for us sinners, now and at the hour of our death. Amen.
7) Hail Mary, full of grace, the Lord is with you! Blessed are you among
women, and blessed is the fruit of thy womb, Jesus. Holy Mary, Mother
of God, pray for us sinners, now and at the hour of our death. Amen.
8) Hail Mary, full of grace, the Lord is with you! Blessed are you among
women, and blessed is the fruit of thy womb, Jesus. Holy Mary, Mother
of God, pray for us sinners, now and at the hour of our death. Amen.
9) Hail Mary, full of grace, the Lord is with you! Blessed are you among
women, and blessed is the fruit of thy womb, Jesus. Holy Mary, Mother
of God, pray for us sinners, now and at the hour of our death. Amen.
10Hail Mary, full of grace, the Lord is with you! Blessed are you among
women, and blessed is the fruit of thy womb, Jesus. Holy Mary, Mother
of God, pray for us sinners, now and at the hour of our death. Amen.

Glory be to the Father, and to the Son, and to the Holy Spirit. As it was
in the beginning is now and ever shall be world without end. Amen
O my Jesus, forgive us our sins, save us from the fire of Hell, lead all
souls to Heaven, especially those who are in most need of your mercy.

2nd Glorious Mystery - The Ascension
Luke 24:36-53

[36] As they were saying this, Jesus himself stood among them, and said to them, "Peace to You." [37] But they were startled and frightened, and supposed that they saw a spirit. [38] And he said to them, "Why are you troubled, and why do questionings rise in your hearts? [39] See my hands and my feet, that it is I myself; handle me, and see; for a spirit has not flesh and bones as you see that I have." [40] And when he had said this he showed them his hands and his feet. [41] And while they still disbelieved for joy, and wondered, he said to them, "Have you anything here to eat?" [42] They gave him a piece of broiled fish, [43] and he took it and ate before them.

[44] Then he said to them, "These are my words which I spoke to you, while I was still with you, that everything written about me in the law of Moses and the prophets and the psalms must be fulfilled." [45] Then he opened their minds to understand the scriptures, [46] and said to them, "Thus it is written, that the Christ should suffer and on the third day rise from the dead, [47] and that repentance and forgiveness of sins should be preached in his name to all nations, beginning from Jerusalem. [48] You are witnesses of these things. [49] And behold, I send the promise of my Father upon you; but stay in the city, until you are clothed with power from on high."

[50] Then he led them out as far as Bethany, and lifting up his hands he blessed them. [51] While he blessed them, he parted from them, and was carried up into heaven. [52] And they worshipped him, and returned to Jerusalem with great joy, [53] and were continually in the temple blessing God.

Our Father, who art in heaven, hallowed be thy name;
thy kingdom come; thy will be done on earth as it is in heaven.
Give us this day our daily bread; and forgive us our trespasses
as we forgive those who trespass against us;
and lead us not into temptation, but deliver us from evil. Amen.

1) Hail Mary, full of grace, the Lord is with you! Blessed are you among women, and blessed is the fruit of thy womb, Jesus. Holy Mary, Mother of God, pray for us sinners, now and at the hour of our death. Amen.
2) Hail Mary, full of grace, the Lord is with you! Blessed are you among women, and blessed is the fruit of thy womb, Jesus. Holy Mary, Mother of God, pray for us sinners, now and at the hour of our death. Amen.
3) Hail Mary, full of grace, the Lord is with you! Blessed are you among women, and blessed is the fruit of thy womb, Jesus. Holy Mary, Mother of God, pray for us sinners, now and at the hour of our death. Amen.
4) Hail Mary, full of grace, the Lord is with you! Blessed are you among women, and blessed is the fruit of thy womb, Jesus. Holy Mary, Mother of God, pray for us sinners, now and at the hour of our death. Amen.
5) Hail Mary, full of grace, the Lord is with you! Blessed are you among women, and blessed is the fruit of thy womb, Jesus. Holy Mary, Mother of God, pray for us sinners, now and at the hour of our death. Amen.

6) Hail Mary, full of grace, the Lord is with you! Blessed are you among women, and blessed is the fruit of thy womb, Jesus. Holy Mary, Mother of God, pray for us sinners, now and at the hour of our death. Amen.
7) Hail Mary, full of grace, the Lord is with you! Blessed are you among women, and blessed is the fruit of thy womb, Jesus. Holy Mary, Mother of God, pray for us sinners, now and at the hour of our death. Amen.
8) Hail Mary, full of grace, the Lord is with you! Blessed are you among women, and blessed is the fruit of thy womb, Jesus. Holy Mary, Mother of God, pray for us sinners, now and at the hour of our death. Amen.
9) Hail Mary, full of grace, the Lord is with you! Blessed are you among women, and blessed is the fruit of thy womb, Jesus. Holy Mary, Mother of God, pray for us sinners, now and at the hour of our death. Amen.
10Hail Mary, full of grace, the Lord is with you! Blessed are you among women, and blessed is the fruit of thy womb, Jesus. Holy Mary, Mother of God, pray for us sinners, now and at the hour of our death. Amen.

Glory be to the Father, and to the Son, and to the Holy Spirit. As it was in the beginning is now and ever shall be world without end. Amen
O my Jesus, forgive us our sins, save us from the fire of Hell, lead all souls to Heaven, especially those who are in most need of your mercy.

3rd Glorious Mystery - The Descent of the Holy Spirit
Acts 2:1-20

[1] When the day of Pentecost had come, they were all together in one place. [2] And suddenly a sound came from heaven like the rush of a mighty wind, and it filled all the house where they were sitting. [3] And there appeared to them tongues as of fire, distributed and resting on each one of them. [4] And they were all filled with the Holy Spirit and began to speak in other tongues, as the Spirit gave them utterance.

[5] Now there were dwelling in Jerusalem Jews, devout men from every nation under heaven. [6] And at this sound the multitude came together, and they were bewildered, because each one heard them speaking in his own language. [7] And they were amazed and wondered, saying, "Are not all these who are speaking Galileans? [8] And how is it that we hear, each of us in his own native language? [9] Parthians and Medes and Elamites and residents of Mesopotamia, Judea and Cappadocia, Pontus and Asia, [10] Phrygia and Pamphylia, Egypt and the parts of Libya belonging to Cyrene, and visitors from Rome, both Jews and proselytes, [11] Cretans and Arabians, we hear them telling in our own tongues the mighty works of God." [12] And all were amazed and perplexed, saying to one another, "What does this mean?" [13] But others mocking said, "They are filled with new wine."

[14] But Peter, standing with the eleven, lifted up his voice and addressed them, "Men of Judea and all who dwell in Jerusalem, let this be known to you, and give ear to my words. [15] For these men are not drunk, as you suppose, since it is only the third hour of the day; [16] but this is what was spoken by the prophet Joel: [17] 'And in the last days it shall be, God declares, that I will pour out my Spirit upon all flesh, and your sons and your daughters shall prophesy, and your young men shall see visions, and your old men shall dream dreams; [18] yea, and on my menservants and my maidservants in those days I will pour out my Spirit; and they shall prophesy. [19] And I will show wonders in the heaven above and signs on the earth beneath, blood, and fire, and vapor of smoke; [20] the sun shall be turned into darkness and the moon into blood, before the day of the Lord comes, the great and manifest day.

Our Father, who art in heaven, hallowed be thy name;
thy kingdom come; thy will be done on earth as it is in heaven.
Give us this day our daily bread; and forgive us our trespasses
as we forgive those who trespass against us;
and lead us not into temptation, but deliver us from evil. Amen.

1) Hail Mary, full of grace, the Lord is with you! Blessed are you among women, and blessed is the fruit of thy womb, Jesus. Holy Mary, Mother of God, pray for us sinners, now and at the hour of our death. Amen.
2) Hail Mary, full of grace, the Lord is with you! Blessed are you among women, and blessed is the fruit of thy womb, Jesus. Holy Mary, Mother of God, pray for us sinners, now and at the hour of our death. Amen.
3) Hail Mary, full of grace, the Lord is with you! Blessed are you among women, and blessed is the fruit of thy womb, Jesus. Holy Mary, Mother of God, pray for us sinners, now and at the hour of our death. Amen.
4) Hail Mary, full of grace, the Lord is with you! Blessed are you among women, and blessed is the fruit of thy womb, Jesus. Holy Mary, Mother of God, pray for us sinners, now and at the hour of our death. Amen.
5) Hail Mary, full of grace, the Lord is with you! Blessed are you among women, and blessed is the fruit of thy womb, Jesus. Holy Mary, Mother of God, pray for us sinners, now and at the hour of our death. Amen.

6) Hail Mary, full of grace, the Lord is with you! Blessed are you among women, and blessed is the fruit of thy womb, Jesus. Holy Mary, Mother of God, pray for us sinners, now and at the hour of our death. Amen.
7) Hail Mary, full of grace, the Lord is with you! Blessed are you among women, and blessed is the fruit of thy womb, Jesus. Holy Mary, Mother of God, pray for us sinners, now and at the hour of our death. Amen.
8) Hail Mary, full of grace, the Lord is with you! Blessed are you among women, and blessed is the fruit of thy womb, Jesus. Holy Mary, Mother of God, pray for us sinners, now and at the hour of our death. Amen.
9) Hail Mary, full of grace, the Lord is with you! Blessed are you among women, and blessed is the fruit of thy womb, Jesus. Holy Mary, Mother of God, pray for us sinners, now and at the hour of our death. Amen.
10Hail Mary, full of grace, the Lord is with you! Blessed are you among women, and blessed is the fruit of thy womb, Jesus. Holy Mary, Mother of God, pray for us sinners, now and at the hour of our death. Amen.

Glory be to the Father, and to the Son, and to the Holy Spirit. As it was in the beginning is now and ever shall be world without end. Amen
O my Jesus, forgive us our sins, save us from the fire of Hell, lead all souls to Heaven, especially those who are in most need of your mercy.

4th Glorious Mystery - The Assumption of Mary

Genesis 3:14-15

[14] The LORD God said to the serpent,
"Because you have done this,
cursed are you above all cattle,
and above all wild animals;
upon your belly you shall go,
and dust you shall eat
all the days of your life.
[15] I will put enmity between you and the woman,
and between your seed and her seed;
he shall bruise your head,
and you shall bruise his heel."

Revelation 12:1

[1] And a great portent appeared in heaven, a woman clothed with the sun, with the moon under her feet, and on her head a crown of twelve stars;

Our Father, who art in heaven, hallowed be thy name;
thy kingdom come; thy will be done on earth as it is in heaven.
Give us this day our daily bread; and forgive us our trespasses
as we forgive those who trespass against us;
and lead us not into temptation, but deliver us from evil. Amen.

1) Hail Mary, full of grace, the Lord is with you! Blessed are you among women, and blessed is the fruit of thy womb, Jesus. Holy Mary, Mother of God, pray for us sinners, now and at the hour of our death. Amen.
2) Hail Mary, full of grace, the Lord is with you! Blessed are you among women, and blessed is the fruit of thy womb, Jesus. Holy Mary, Mother of God, pray for us sinners, now and at the hour of our death. Amen.
3) Hail Mary, full of grace, the Lord is with you! Blessed are you among women, and blessed is the fruit of thy womb, Jesus. Holy Mary, Mother of God, pray for us sinners, now and at the hour of our death. Amen.
4) Hail Mary, full of grace, the Lord is with you! Blessed are you among women, and blessed is the fruit of thy womb, Jesus. Holy Mary, Mother of God, pray for us sinners, now and at the hour of our death. Amen.
5) Hail Mary, full of grace, the Lord is with you! Blessed are you among women, and blessed is the fruit of thy womb, Jesus. Holy Mary, Mother of God, pray for us sinners, now and at the hour of our death. Amen.

6) Hail Mary, full of grace, the Lord is with you! Blessed are you among women, and blessed is the fruit of thy womb, Jesus. Holy Mary, Mother of God, pray for us sinners, now and at the hour of our death. Amen.
7) Hail Mary, full of grace, the Lord is with you! Blessed are you among women, and blessed is the fruit of thy womb, Jesus. Holy Mary, Mother of God, pray for us sinners, now and at the hour of our death. Amen.
8) Hail Mary, full of grace, the Lord is with you! Blessed are you among women, and blessed is the fruit of thy womb, Jesus. Holy Mary, Mother of God, pray for us sinners, now and at the hour of our death. Amen.
9) Hail Mary, full of grace, the Lord is with you! Blessed are you among women, and blessed is the fruit of thy womb, Jesus. Holy Mary, Mother of God, pray for us sinners, now and at the hour of our death. Amen.
10 Hail Mary, full of grace, the Lord is with you! Blessed are you among women, and blessed is the fruit of thy womb, Jesus. Holy Mary, Mother of God, pray for us sinners, now and at the hour of our death. Amen.

Glory be to the Father, and to the Son, and to the Holy Spirit. As it was in the beginning is now and ever shall be world without end. Amen
O my Jesus, forgive us our sins, save us from the fire of Hell, lead all souls to Heaven, especially those who are in most need of your mercy.

5th Glorious Mystery - The Coronation of Mary

Judith 15:9-10

9 And when they met her they all blessed her with one accord and said to her, "You are the exaltation of Jerusalem, you are the great glory of Israel, you are the great pride of our nation! 10 You have done all this singlehanded; you have done great good to Israel, and God is well pleased with it. May the Almighty Lord bless you for ever!" And all the people said, "So be it!"

Luke 1:46-49

46 And Mary said, "My soul magnifies the Lord, 47 and my spirit rejoices in God my Savior, 48 for he has regarded the low estate of his handmaiden. For behold, henceforth all generations will call me blessed; 49 for he who is mighty has done great things for me, and holy is his name.

Our Father, who art in heaven, hallowed be thy name;
thy kingdom come; thy will be done on earth as it is in heaven.
Give us this day our daily bread; and forgive us our trespasses
as we forgive those who trespass against us;
and lead us not into temptation, but deliver us from evil. Amen.

1) Hail Mary, full of grace, the Lord is with you! Blessed are you among
women, and blessed is the fruit of thy womb, Jesus. Holy Mary, Mother
of God, pray for us sinners, now and at the hour of our death. Amen.
2) Hail Mary, full of grace, the Lord is with you! Blessed are you among
women, and blessed is the fruit of thy womb, Jesus. Holy Mary, Mother
of God, pray for us sinners, now and at the hour of our death. Amen.
3) Hail Mary, full of grace, the Lord is with you! Blessed are you among
women, and blessed is the fruit of thy womb, Jesus. Holy Mary, Mother
of God, pray for us sinners, now and at the hour of our death. Amen.
4) Hail Mary, full of grace, the Lord is with you! Blessed are you among
women, and blessed is the fruit of thy womb, Jesus. Holy Mary, Mother
of God, pray for us sinners, now and at the hour of our death. Amen.
5) Hail Mary, full of grace, the Lord is with you! Blessed are you among
women, and blessed is the fruit of thy womb, Jesus. Holy Mary, Mother
of God, pray for us sinners, now and at the hour of our death. Amen.

6) Hail Mary, full of grace, the Lord is with you! Blessed are you among
women, and blessed is the fruit of thy womb, Jesus. Holy Mary, Mother
of God, pray for us sinners, now and at the hour of our death. Amen.
7) Hail Mary, full of grace, the Lord is with you! Blessed are you among
women, and blessed is the fruit of thy womb, Jesus. Holy Mary, Mother
of God, pray for us sinners, now and at the hour of our death. Amen.
8) Hail Mary, full of grace, the Lord is with you! Blessed are you among
women, and blessed is the fruit of thy womb, Jesus. Holy Mary, Mother
of God, pray for us sinners, now and at the hour of our death. Amen.
9) Hail Mary, full of grace, the Lord is with you! Blessed are you among
women, and blessed is the fruit of thy womb, Jesus. Holy Mary, Mother
of God, pray for us sinners, now and at the hour of our death. Amen.
10Hail Mary, full of grace, the Lord is with you! Blessed are you among
women, and blessed is the fruit of thy womb, Jesus. Holy Mary, Mother
of God, pray for us sinners, now and at the hour of our death. Amen.

Glory be to the Father, and to the Son, and to the Holy Spirit. As it was
in the beginning is now and ever shall be world without end. Amen
O my Jesus, forgive us our sins, save us from the fire of Hell, lead all
souls to Heaven, especially those who are in most need of your mercy.

FRANCE

O MARIE CONÇUE SANS
PÉCHÉ PRIEZ POUR NOUS QUI AVONS
RECOURS À VOUS

ANNO

8) *The Five Luminous Mysteries on Thursdays*

1st Luminous Mystery - The Baptism of Christ in the Jordan
Matthew 3:11-17

[11] "I baptize you with water for repentance, but he who is coming after me is mightier than I, whose sandals I am not worthy to carry; he will baptize you with the Holy Spirit and with fire. [12] His winnowing fork is in his hand, and he will clear his threshing floor and gather his wheat into the granary, but the chaff he will burn with unquenchable fire."

[13] Then Jesus came from Galilee to the Jordan to John, to be baptized by him. [14] John would have prevented him, saying, "I need to be baptized by you, and do you come to me?" [15] But Jesus answered him, "Let it be so now; for thus it is fitting for us to fulfil all righteousness." Then he consented. [16] And when Jesus was baptized, he went up immediately from the water, and behold, the heavens were opened and he saw the Spirit of God descending like a dove, and alighting on him; [17] and lo, a voice from heaven, saying, "This is my beloved Son, with whom I am well pleased."

Our Father, who art in heaven, hallowed be thy name;
thy kingdom come; thy will be done on earth as it is in heaven.
Give us this day our daily bread; and forgive us our trespasses
as we forgive those who trespass against us;
and lead us not into temptation, but deliver us from evil. Amen.

1) Hail Mary, full of grace, the Lord is with you! Blessed are you among women, and blessed is the fruit of thy womb, Jesus. Holy Mary, Mother of God, pray for us sinners, now and at the hour of our death. Amen.
2) Hail Mary, full of grace, the Lord is with you! Blessed are you among women, and blessed is the fruit of thy womb, Jesus. Holy Mary, Mother of God, pray for us sinners, now and at the hour of our death. Amen.
3) Hail Mary, full of grace, the Lord is with you! Blessed are you among women, and blessed is the fruit of thy womb, Jesus. Holy Mary, Mother of God, pray for us sinners, now and at the hour of our death. Amen.
4) Hail Mary, full of grace, the Lord is with you! Blessed are you among women, and blessed is the fruit of thy womb, Jesus. Holy Mary, Mother of God, pray for us sinners, now and at the hour of our death. Amen.
5) Hail Mary, full of grace, the Lord is with you! Blessed are you among women, and blessed is the fruit of thy womb, Jesus. Holy Mary, Mother of God, pray for us sinners, now and at the hour of our death. Amen.

6) Hail Mary, full of grace, the Lord is with you! Blessed are you among women, and blessed is the fruit of thy womb, Jesus. Holy Mary, Mother of God, pray for us sinners, now and at the hour of our death. Amen.
7) Hail Mary, full of grace, the Lord is with you! Blessed are you among women, and blessed is the fruit of thy womb, Jesus. Holy Mary, Mother of God, pray for us sinners, now and at the hour of our death. Amen.
8) Hail Mary, full of grace, the Lord is with you! Blessed are you among women, and blessed is the fruit of thy womb, Jesus. Holy Mary, Mother of God, pray for us sinners, now and at the hour of our death. Amen.
9) Hail Mary, full of grace, the Lord is with you! Blessed are you among women, and blessed is the fruit of thy womb, Jesus. Holy Mary, Mother of God, pray for us sinners, now and at the hour of our death. Amen.
10Hail Mary, full of grace, the Lord is with you! Blessed are you among women, and blessed is the fruit of thy womb, Jesus. Holy Mary, Mother of God, pray for us sinners, now and at the hour of our death. Amen.

Glory be to the Father, and to the Son, and to the Holy Spirit. As it was in the beginning is now and ever shall be world without end. Amen
O my Jesus, forgive us our sins, save us from the fire of Hell, lead all souls to Heaven, especially those who are in most need of your mercy.

2nd Luminous Mystery - The Wedding Feast at Cana
John 2:1-12

[1] On the third day there was a marriage at Cana in Galilee, and the mother of Jesus was there; [2] Jesus also was invited to the marriage, with his disciples. [3] When the wine failed, the mother of Jesus said to him, "They have no wine." [4] And Jesus said to her, "O woman, what have you to do with me? My hour has not yet come." [5] His mother said to the servants, "Do whatever he tells you." [6] Now six stone jars were standing there, for the Jewish rites of purification, each holding twenty or thirty gallons. [7] Jesus said to them, "Fill the jars with water." And they filled them up to the brim. [8] He said to them, "Now draw some out, and take it to the steward of the feast." So they took it. [9] When the steward of the feast tasted the water now become wine, and did not know where it came from (though the servants who had drawn the water knew), the steward of the feast called the bridegroom [10] and said to him, "Every man serves the good wine first; and when men have drunk freely, then the poor wine; but you have kept the good wine until now." [11] This, the first of his signs, Jesus did at Cana in Galilee, and manifested his glory; and his disciples believed in him.

[12] After this he went down to Caperna-um, with his mother and his brethern and his disciples; and there they stayed for a few days.

Our Father, who art in heaven, hallowed be thy name;
thy kingdom come; thy will be done on earth as it is in heaven.
Give us this day our daily bread; and forgive us our trespasses
as we forgive those who trespass against us;
and lead us not into temptation, but deliver us from evil. Amen.

1) Hail Mary, full of grace, the Lord is with you! Blessed are you among
women, and blessed is the fruit of thy womb, Jesus. Holy Mary, Mother
of God, pray for us sinners, now and at the hour of our death. Amen.
2) Hail Mary, full of grace, the Lord is with you! Blessed are you among
women, and blessed is the fruit of thy womb, Jesus. Holy Mary, Mother
of God, pray for us sinners, now and at the hour of our death. Amen.
3) Hail Mary, full of grace, the Lord is with you! Blessed are you among
women, and blessed is the fruit of thy womb, Jesus. Holy Mary, Mother
of God, pray for us sinners, now and at the hour of our death. Amen.
4) Hail Mary, full of grace, the Lord is with you! Blessed are you among
women, and blessed is the fruit of thy womb, Jesus. Holy Mary, Mother
of God, pray for us sinners, now and at the hour of our death. Amen.
5) Hail Mary, full of grace, the Lord is with you! Blessed are you among
women, and blessed is the fruit of thy womb, Jesus. Holy Mary, Mother
of God, pray for us sinners, now and at the hour of our death. Amen.

6) Hail Mary, full of grace, the Lord is with you! Blessed are you among
women, and blessed is the fruit of thy womb, Jesus. Holy Mary, Mother
of God, pray for us sinners, now and at the hour of our death. Amen.
7) Hail Mary, full of grace, the Lord is with you! Blessed are you among
women, and blessed is the fruit of thy womb, Jesus. Holy Mary, Mother
of God, pray for us sinners, now and at the hour of our death. Amen.
8) Hail Mary, full of grace, the Lord is with you! Blessed are you among
women, and blessed is the fruit of thy womb, Jesus. Holy Mary, Mother
of God, pray for us sinners, now and at the hour of our death. Amen.
9) Hail Mary, full of grace, the Lord is with you! Blessed are you among
women, and blessed is the fruit of thy womb, Jesus. Holy Mary, Mother
of God, pray for us sinners, now and at the hour of our death. Amen.
10Hail Mary, full of grace, the Lord is with you! Blessed are you among
women, and blessed is the fruit of thy womb, Jesus. Holy Mary, Mother
of God, pray for us sinners, now and at the hour of our death. Amen.

Glory be to the Father, and to the Son, and to the Holy Spirit. As it was
in the beginning is now and ever shall be world without end. Amen
O my Jesus, forgive us our sins, save us from the fire of Hell, lead all
souls to Heaven, especially those who are in most need of your mercy.

3rd Luminous Mystery - Proclamation of the Kingdom of God
Mark 1:1-15

[1] The beginning of the gospel of Jesus Christ, the Son of God. [2] As it is written in Isaiah the prophet, "Behold, I send my messenger before thy face, who shall prepare thy way; [3] the voice of one crying in the wilderness: Prepare the way of the Lord, make his paths straight—" [4] John the baptizer appeared in the wilderness, preaching a baptism of repentance for the forgiveness of sins. [5] And there went out to him all the country of Judea, and all the people of Jerusalem; and they were baptized by him in the river Jordan, confessing their sins. [6] Now John was clothed with camel's hair, and had a leather girdle around his waist, and ate locusts and wild honey. [7] And he preached, saying, "After me comes he who is mightier than I, the thong of whose sandals I am not worthy to stoop down and untie. [8] I have baptized you with water; but he will baptize you with the Holy Spirit."

[9] In those days Jesus came from Nazareth of Galilee and was baptized by John in the Jordan. [10] And when he came up out of the water, immediately he saw the heavens opened and the Spirit descending upon him like a dove; [11] and a voice came from heaven, "Thou art my beloved Son; with thee I am well pleased."

[12] The Spirit immediately drove him out into the wilderness. [13] And he was in the wilderness forty days, tempted by Satan; and he was with the wild beasts; and the angels ministered to him.

[14] Now after John was arrested, Jesus came into Galilee, preaching the gospel of God, [15] and saying, "The time is fulfilled, and the kingdom of God is at hand; repent, and believe in the gospel."

Our Father, who art in heaven, hallowed be thy name;
thy kingdom come; thy will be done on earth as it is in heaven.
Give us this day our daily bread; and forgive us our trespasses
as we forgive those who trespass against us;
and lead us not into temptation, but deliver us from evil. Amen.

1) Hail Mary, full of grace, the Lord is with you! Blessed are you among women, and blessed is the fruit of thy womb, Jesus. Holy Mary, Mother of God, pray for us sinners, now and at the hour of our death. Amen.
2) Hail Mary, full of grace, the Lord is with you! Blessed are you among women, and blessed is the fruit of thy womb, Jesus. Holy Mary, Mother of God, pray for us sinners, now and at the hour of our death. Amen.
3) Hail Mary, full of grace, the Lord is with you! Blessed are you among women, and blessed is the fruit of thy womb, Jesus. Holy Mary, Mother of God, pray for us sinners, now and at the hour of our death. Amen.
4) Hail Mary, full of grace, the Lord is with you! Blessed are you among women, and blessed is the fruit of thy womb, Jesus. Holy Mary, Mother of God, pray for us sinners, now and at the hour of our death. Amen.
5) Hail Mary, full of grace, the Lord is with you! Blessed are you among women, and blessed is the fruit of thy womb, Jesus. Holy Mary, Mother of God, pray for us sinners, now and at the hour of our death. Amen.

6) Hail Mary, full of grace, the Lord is with you! Blessed are you among women, and blessed is the fruit of thy womb, Jesus. Holy Mary, Mother of God, pray for us sinners, now and at the hour of our death. Amen.
7) Hail Mary, full of grace, the Lord is with you! Blessed are you among women, and blessed is the fruit of thy womb, Jesus. Holy Mary, Mother of God, pray for us sinners, now and at the hour of our death. Amen.
8) Hail Mary, full of grace, the Lord is with you! Blessed are you among women, and blessed is the fruit of thy womb, Jesus. Holy Mary, Mother of God, pray for us sinners, now and at the hour of our death. Amen.
9) Hail Mary, full of grace, the Lord is with you! Blessed are you among women, and blessed is the fruit of thy womb, Jesus. Holy Mary, Mother of God, pray for us sinners, now and at the hour of our death. Amen.
10Hail Mary, full of grace, the Lord is with you! Blessed are you among women, and blessed is the fruit of thy womb, Jesus. Holy Mary, Mother of God, pray for us sinners, now and at the hour of our death. Amen.

Glory be to the Father, and to the Son, and to the Holy Spirit. As it was in the beginning is now and ever shall be world without end. Amen
O my Jesus, forgive us our sins, save us from the fire of Hell, lead all souls to Heaven, especially those who are in most need of your mercy.

4th Luminous Mystery - The Transfiguration
Matthew 17:1-13

[1] And after six days Jesus took with him Peter and James and John his brother, and led them up a high mountain apart. [2] And he was transfigured before them, and his face shone like the sun, and his garments became white as light. [3] And behold, there appeared to them Moses and Elijah, talking with him. [4] And Peter said to Jesus, "Lord, it is well that we are here; if you wish, I will make three booths here, one for you and one for Moses and one for Elijah." [5] He was still speaking, when lo, a bright cloud overshadowed them, and a voice from the cloud said, "This is my beloved Son, with whom I am well pleased; listen to him." [6] When the disciples heard this, they fell on their faces, and were filled with awe. [7] But Jesus came and touched them, saying, "Rise, and have no fear." [8] And when they lifted up their eyes, they saw no one but Jesus only.

[9] And as they were coming down the mountain, Jesus commanded them, "Tell no one the vision, until the Son of man is raised from the dead." [10] And the disciples asked him, "Then why do the scribes say that first Elijah must come?" [11] He replied, "Elijah does come, and he is to restore all things; [12] but I tell you that Elijah has already come, and they did not know him, but did to him whatever they pleased. So also the Son of man will suffer at their hands." [13] Then the disciples understood that he was speaking to them of John the Baptist.

Our Father, who art in heaven, hallowed be thy name;
thy kingdom come; thy will be done on earth as it is in heaven.
Give us this day our daily bread; and forgive us our trespasses
as we forgive those who trespass against us;
and lead us not into temptation, but deliver us from evil. Amen.

1) Hail Mary, full of grace, the Lord is with you! Blessed are you among women, and blessed is the fruit of thy womb, Jesus. Holy Mary, Mother of God, pray for us sinners, now and at the hour of our death. Amen.
2) Hail Mary, full of grace, the Lord is with you! Blessed are you among women, and blessed is the fruit of thy womb, Jesus. Holy Mary, Mother of God, pray for us sinners, now and at the hour of our death. Amen.
3) Hail Mary, full of grace, the Lord is with you! Blessed are you among women, and blessed is the fruit of thy womb, Jesus. Holy Mary, Mother of God, pray for us sinners, now and at the hour of our death. Amen.
4) Hail Mary, full of grace, the Lord is with you! Blessed are you among women, and blessed is the fruit of thy womb, Jesus. Holy Mary, Mother of God, pray for us sinners, now and at the hour of our death. Amen.
5) Hail Mary, full of grace, the Lord is with you! Blessed are you among women, and blessed is the fruit of thy womb, Jesus. Holy Mary, Mother of God, pray for us sinners, now and at the hour of our death. Amen.

6) Hail Mary, full of grace, the Lord is with you! Blessed are you among women, and blessed is the fruit of thy womb, Jesus. Holy Mary, Mother of God, pray for us sinners, now and at the hour of our death. Amen.
7) Hail Mary, full of grace, the Lord is with you! Blessed are you among women, and blessed is the fruit of thy womb, Jesus. Holy Mary, Mother of God, pray for us sinners, now and at the hour of our death. Amen.
8) Hail Mary, full of grace, the Lord is with you! Blessed are you among women, and blessed is the fruit of thy womb, Jesus. Holy Mary, Mother of God, pray for us sinners, now and at the hour of our death. Amen.
9) Hail Mary, full of grace, the Lord is with you! Blessed are you among women, and blessed is the fruit of thy womb, Jesus. Holy Mary, Mother of God, pray for us sinners, now and at the hour of our death. Amen.
10Hail Mary, full of grace, the Lord is with you! Blessed are you among women, and blessed is the fruit of thy womb, Jesus. Holy Mary, Mother of God, pray for us sinners, now and at the hour of our death. Amen.

Glory be to the Father, and to the Son, and to the Holy Spirit. As it was in the beginning is now and ever shall be world without end. Amen
O my Jesus, forgive us our sins, save us from the fire of Hell, lead all souls to Heaven, especially those who are in most need of your mercy.

5th Luminous Mystery - The Institution of the Eucharist
Luke 22:7-20

[7] Then came the day of Unleavened Bread, on which the passover lamb had to be sacrificed. [8] So Jesus sent Peter and John, saying, "Go and prepare the passover for us, that we may eat it." [9] They said to him, "Where will you have us prepare it?" [10] He said to them, "Behold, when you have entered the city, a man carrying a jar of water will meet you; follow him into the house which he enters, [11] and tell the householder, 'The Teacher says to you, Where is the guest room, where I am to eat the passover with my disciples?' [12] And he will show you a large upper room furnished; there make ready." [13] And they went, and found it as he had told them; and they prepared the passover.

[14] And when the hour came, he sat at table, and the apostles with him. [15] And he said to them, "I have earnestly desired to eat this passover with you before I suffer; [16] for I tell you I shall not eat it until it is fulfilled in the kingdom of God." [17] And he took a cup, and when he had given thanks he said, "Take this, and divide it among yourselves; [18] for I tell you that from now on I shall not drink of the fruit of the vine until the kingdom of God comes." [19] And he took bread, and when he had given thanks he broke it and gave it to them, saying, "This is my body which is given for you. Do this in remembrance of me." [20] And likewise the cup after supper, saying, "This cup which is poured out for you is the new covenant in my blood.

Our Father, who art in heaven, hallowed be thy name;
thy kingdom come; thy will be done on earth as it is in heaven.
Give us this day our daily bread; and forgive us our trespasses
as we forgive those who trespass against us;
and lead us not into temptation, but deliver us from evil. Amen.

1) Hail Mary, full of grace, the Lord is with you! Blessed are you among women, and blessed is the fruit of thy womb, Jesus. Holy Mary, Mother of God, pray for us sinners, now and at the hour of our death. Amen.
2) Hail Mary, full of grace, the Lord is with you! Blessed are you among women, and blessed is the fruit of thy womb, Jesus. Holy Mary, Mother of God, pray for us sinners, now and at the hour of our death. Amen.
3) Hail Mary, full of grace, the Lord is with you! Blessed are you among women, and blessed is the fruit of thy womb, Jesus. Holy Mary, Mother of God, pray for us sinners, now and at the hour of our death. Amen.
4) Hail Mary, full of grace, the Lord is with you! Blessed are you among women, and blessed is the fruit of thy womb, Jesus. Holy Mary, Mother of God, pray for us sinners, now and at the hour of our death. Amen.
5) Hail Mary, full of grace, the Lord is with you! Blessed are you among women, and blessed is the fruit of thy womb, Jesus. Holy Mary, Mother of God, pray for us sinners, now and at the hour of our death. Amen.

6) Hail Mary, full of grace, the Lord is with you! Blessed are you among women, and blessed is the fruit of thy womb, Jesus. Holy Mary, Mother of God, pray for us sinners, now and at the hour of our death. Amen.
7) Hail Mary, full of grace, the Lord is with you! Blessed are you among women, and blessed is the fruit of thy womb, Jesus. Holy Mary, Mother of God, pray for us sinners, now and at the hour of our death. Amen.
8) Hail Mary, full of grace, the Lord is with you! Blessed are you among women, and blessed is the fruit of thy womb, Jesus. Holy Mary, Mother of God, pray for us sinners, now and at the hour of our death. Amen.
9) Hail Mary, full of grace, the Lord is with you! Blessed are you among women, and blessed is the fruit of thy womb, Jesus. Holy Mary, Mother of God, pray for us sinners, now and at the hour of our death. Amen.
10Hail Mary, full of grace, the Lord is with you! Blessed are you among women, and blessed is the fruit of thy womb, Jesus. Holy Mary, Mother of God, pray for us sinners, now and at the hour of our death. Amen.

Glory be to the Father, and to the Son, and to the Holy Spirit. As it was in the beginning is now and ever shall be world without end. Amen
O my Jesus, forgive us our sins, save us from the fire of Hell, lead all souls to Heaven, especially those who are in most need of your mercy.

9) Ending Rosary Prayers

Hail, holy Queen, mother of mercy,
our life, our sweetness, and our hope.
To you do we cry,
poor, banished children of Eve.
To you we send up our sighs
mourning and weeping in this vale of tears.
Turn then, most gracious advocate,
your eyes of mercy toward us,
and after this exile
show unto us the blessed fruit of your womb, Jesus.
O clement, O loving,
O sweet Virgin Mary.

Pray for us, O holy Mother of God,
that we may be made worthy of the promises of Christ.

In the name of the Father, and of the Son, and of the Holy Spirit.
Amen.

10) Rosary Prayers Collection

Sign of the Cross
In the name of the Father, and of the Son, and of the Holy Spirit.
Amen.

Apostles' Creed
I believe in God, the Father almighty, Creator of heaven and earth.
and in Jesus Christ, his only Son, Our Lord.
who was conceived by the Holy Spirit, born of the Virgin Mary,
suffered under Pontius Pilate, was crucified, died and was buried;
he descended into hell;
on the third day he rose again from the dead;
he ascended into heaven,
and is seated at the right hand of God the Father almighty;
from there he will come to judge the living and the dead.
I believe in the Holy Spirit, the holy catholic Church,
the communion of saints, the forgiveness of sins,
the resurrection of the body, and life everlasting. Amen.

Our Father (Lord's Prayer)
Our Father, who art in heaven,
hallowed be thy name;
thy kingdom come;
thy will be done on earth as it is in heaven.
Give us this day our daily bread;
and forgive us our trespasses
as we forgive those who trespass against us;
and lead us not into temptation,
but deliver us from evil. Amen

Hail Mary
Hail Mary, full of grace,
the Lord is with you!
Blessed are you among women,
and blessed is the fruit of your womb, Jesus.
Holy Mary, Mother of God,
pray for us sinners,
now and at the hour of our death. Amen.

Glory Be (Doxology)

Glory be to the Father,
and to the Son,
and to the Holy Spirit.
As it was in the beginning,
is now, and ever shall be
world without end.
Amen

O My Jesus (Fatima Prayer)

O my Jesus, forgive us our sins,
save us from the fire of Hell,
lead all souls to Heaven,
especially those who are in most need of your mercy.

Hail Holy Queen (Salve Regina)

Hail, holy Queen, mother of mercy,
our life, our sweetness, and our hope.
To you do we cry,
poor, banished children of Eve.
To you we send up our sighs
mourning and weeping in this vale of tears.
Turn then, most gracious advocate,
your eyes of mercy toward us,
and after this exile
show unto us the blessed fruit of your womb, Jesus.
O clement, O loving,
O sweet Virgin Mary.

Pray for us, O holy Mother of God,
that we may be made worthy of the promises of Christ.

11) Rosary Prayers Gospel Sources

Our Father (Lord's Prayer)
Our Father, who art in heaven,
hallowed be thy name; thy kingdom come;
thy will be done on earth as it is in heaven.
Give us this day our daily bread;
and forgive us our trespasses
as we forgive those who trespass against us;
and lead us not into temptation,
but deliver us from evil. Amen

Luke 11

[1] He was praying in a certain place, and when he ceased, one of his disciples said to him, "Lord, teach us to pray, as John taught his disciples." [2] And he said to them, "When you pray, say:
"Father, hallowed be thy name. Thy kingdom come.
[3] Give us each day our daily bread; [4] and forgive us our sins, for we ourselves forgive every one who is indebted to us; and lead us not into temptation."

Matthew 6

[5] "And when you pray, you must not be like the hypocrites; for they love to stand and pray in the synagogues and at the street corners, that they may be seen by men. Truly, I say to you, they have received their reward. [6] But when you pray, go into your room and shut the door and pray to your Father who is in secret; and your Father who sees in secret will reward you.
[7] "And in praying do not heap up empty phrases as the Gentiles do; for they think that they will be heard for their many words. [8] Do not be like them, for your Father knows what you need before you ask him. [9] Pray then like this: Our Father who art in heaven, Hallowed be thy name. [10] Thy kingdom come. Thy will be done, On earth as it is in heaven. [11] Give us this day our daily bread; [12] And forgive us our debts, As we also have forgiven our debtors; [13] And lead us not into temptation, But deliver us from evil.

Hail Mary
Hail Mary, full of grace,
the Lord is with you!
Blessed are you among women,
and blessed is the fruit of your womb, Jesus.
Holy Mary, Mother of God,
pray for us sinners,
now and at the hour of our death. Amen.

Luke 1

26 In the sixth month the angel Gabriel was sent from God to a city of Galilee named Nazareth, 27 to a virgin betrothed to a man whose name was Joseph, of the house of David; and the virgin's name was Mary. 28 And he came to her and said, "Hail, full of grace, the Lord is with you!"

39 In those days Mary arose and went with haste into the hill country, to a city of Judah, 40 and she entered the house of Zechariah and greeted Elizabeth. 41 And when Elizabeth heard the greeting of Mary, the babe leaped in her womb; and Elizabeth was filled with the Holy Spirit 42 and she exclaimed with a loud cry, "Blessed are you among women, and blessed is the fruit of your womb! 43 And why is this granted me, that the mother of my Lord should come to me?

12) Shrine Donations

From the very beginning, the Sanctuary of Our Lady of Lourdes always sought to welcome pilgrims under the most favourable conditions. Churches were built to provide places where the faithful could pray, the Accommodation for the Sick was constructed to provide shelter for the sick and disabled pilgrims. Today the Sanctuary of Our Lady of Lourdes continues to invest in this ideal. These investments can only be made through your generosity.

To help, you can send a donation by credit card:
http://www.lourdes-france.org/index.php?goto_centre=ru&contexte=en&id=774

or by check, made payable to:
"Association Diocésaine de Tarbes et Lourdes".
Please send it to the following address and include your name and address, as well as your reason for sending your donation:
Association Diocésaine de Tarbes et Lourdes
Service de traitement des dons par internet
1 Av. Mgr Théas
65108 Lourdes Cedex, France

Shrine Contact Info
The Sanctuary :
1, avenue Monseigneur Théas
65108 LOURDES CEDEX, FRANCE
Tél. 33 (0) 5 62 42 78 78
Fax. 33 (0) 5 62 42 78 77
http://www.lourdes-france.org

HOLY BIBLE

INRI

Credits

Book by Laus Deo Publishing
Cover Photo by jozef sedmak/Photos.com, Page # Photos by
8-Ed Chambers/Photos.com, 9-Antonio Ribeiro/Photos.com,
10-Tiago Estima/Photos.com, 12-Mark Kimmet/Photos.com,
14T-Serge Villa/Photos.com, 14B-tamer yazici/Photos.com,
17-jozef sedmak/Photos.com, 41-Francisco Javier Gil Oreja/Photos.com, 53-
Antonio Ribeiro/Photos.com,
71-Shane Cummins/Photos.com
T=Top, B=Bottom, R=Right, L=Left

Copyrights

Our Lady of Lourdes by Georges Bertrin, Catholic Encyclopedia 2013. LASSERRE, Notre-Dame de Lourdes; BOISSARIE, L'oeuvre de Lourdes; BERTRIN, Histoire critique des événements de Lourdes, apparitions et guérisons (Paris, 1909), tr. GIBBS; IDEM, Un miracle d'aujourd'hui avec une radiographie (Paris, 1909).

Made in the USA
San Bernardino, CA
10 December 2016